THE HISTORY DETECTIVE INVESTIGATES

The Civil Wars

Simon Adams

WAYLAND

First published in 2008 by Wayland

Copyright © Wayland 2008

Wayland
338 Euston Road
London NW1 3BH

Wayland Australia
Level 17/207 Kent Street
Sydney, NSW 2000

Editor: Camilla Lloyd
Designer: Simon Burrough
Picture Researcher: Shelley Noronha

Picture Acknowledgments: The author and publisher would like to thank the following for their pictures to be reproduced in this publication: Cover photographs: Wayland Picture Library (both); AKG: Sotheby's/akg-images: 24; The Art Archive: British Museum/Eileen Tweedy: 4, The Art Archive: 7, 26, 27 (t); Getty Images: altrendo images: 9 (b); Peter Hicks: 14 (b), 15, 17 (b), 21; Topfoto: 6, 9 (t), 12 (t), 13, 14 (t), 16, 17, (t), 18, 19 (b), Fotomas/Topfoto: 8, 10, 11 (t), 20, 22, 23, 25, National Pictures/Topfoto: 27 (b), Print Collect/HIP/Topfoto: 28, Print Collector/HIP/Topfoto: 12 (b), Roger-Viollet/Topfoto: 29, WHA/Topfoto: 11 (b); Wayland Picture Library: 1, 5, 7, 19, 20 (t).

British Library Cataloguing in Publication Data:
Adams, Simon, 1955-
 The Civil Wars. - (The history detective investigates)
 1. Great Britain - History - Civil War, 1642-1649
Juvenile literature 2. Great Britain - History - Commonwealth and Protectorate, 1649
1660 - Juvenile literature
I. Title
942'.062

ISBN: 978 0 7502 5340 6

Printed in China

Wayland is a division of Hachette Children's Books, an Hachette Livre UK company

Contents

Words in **bold** can be found in the glossary on page 30

The history detective Sherlock Bones, will help you to find clues and collect evidence about the civil wars. Wherever you see one of Sherlock's paw-prints, you will find a mystery to solve. The answers can be found on page 31.

What caused the civil wars?

In 1637, conflict broke out in Scotland and soon spread across the whole of the British Isles. England and Wales, Scotland, and Ireland were gripped by a series of civil wars that eventually led to the execution of the king in 1649 and the establishment of a republic that lasted until 1660. These wars have been called the Wars of the Three Kingdoms and also the English Civil War, as most of the fighting took place in England. What brought about these civil wars?

In 1625, Charles I became king. Charles ruled three kingdoms – England and Wales, Scotland, and Ireland – each with its own government, parliament, laws, and religion. The Church of England was **Protestant** and was run by bishops appointed by the king, who was head of the church. Many people, however, were **Puritans** who wanted to worship in their own, more simple way, or **Independents** who disliked the established official church. Scotland had its own Protestant church, the **Presbyterian** Kirk, in which church members elected their own presbyters (ministers) instead. Most people in Ireland were members of the **Roman Catholic Church**.

Charles had very strong religious views and wanted to force the Church of England and its bishops on both Scotland and Ireland against their will. Charles also believed he had been given a divine right to rule by God and that he was answerable only to God for what he did and not to his people, their parliaments or their churches.

 Why was this area of London known as Whitehall?

DETECTIVE WORK

Charles I's father, James I, was the first Stuart king. Under his rule, the two thrones of Scotland and England were combined under one king for the first time. Find out who the Stuart kings were, and where they came from. Make a list of them, with the dates of their reigns, starting with James I in 1603. This website will help you: http://www.royal.gov.uk

Whitehall, a part of London, in the mid-17th century, as painted by Wenceslaus Hollar.

White Hall   Palatium Regis

From 1629 onwards, Charles refused to call the English parliament and ruled without it. However, parliament alone still had the power to raise taxes. Charles could not simply raise taxes himself, as he had to call and consult parliament in order to do this.

When Charles tried to introduce his religious policies in Scotland, the country rose in revolt. Charles was, therefore, forced in 1640, to recall the English parliament to raise money to fund an army to fight the Scots. Many Members of Parliament (**MPs**) opposed the king and wanted to restrict his powers. In 1641, Irish Catholics too rose in revolt against Protestant settlers taking their land. With two of his three kingdoms in chaos, Charles tried but failed to arrest five leading MPs who were opposed to him. The civil wars now spread from Scotland and Ireland to England.

Charles I was painted by Daniel Mytens in 1628.

'*Men wondered that so good a man should be so bad a king.*'

At the end of his life, and his reign, the wife of one of the signatories of Charles I's death warrant, pointed out the huge contrast between the shy and charming man devoted to his wife and family, and the arrogant, quarrelsome man who was king.

Who supported the king?

When the civil war broke out in England in 1642, people took sides – for or against Charles I – just as they had in Scotland and Ireland. There were lots of reasons why people chose to support the king.

In the 1600s, almost every country in Europe had a king. People in the British Isles had never known a different form of government. The king was the head of the country and people followed him and were loyal to him because they looked up to him as the king. Others followed him because they believed in order and authority, and the king represented both. They believed he had the divine right to rule, and they accepted his rule without question.

Most members of the nobility – dukes, earls and others – and the rich landed gentry supported him because many owed their position in society and their lands to him. The nobility, like the king, passed their titles, their lands and power down in the **hereditary** way from father to son. They believed in the hereditary right to rule, and disliked elected government by parliament.

The Cavaliers were often mounted on horseback and bravely supported the king.

'Brother, what I feared is proved to be true, which is your being against the King; give me leave to tell you in my opinion "tis most unhandsomely done, and it grieves my heart to think that my father already and I, who so dearly love and esteem you, should be bound to be your enemy. I hear 'tis a great grief to my father.'"

Edmund Verney writing to his elder brother Ralph Verney MP. The civil wars even divided families, as this letter shows.

This Cavalier is dressed in the fashionable style of the time and is carrying a sword.

The king drew support from members of the Church of England, and from Roman Catholics, even though the Catholics in Ireland were in revolt against the king. Charles's French wife, Henrietta Maria, was Catholic, and many suspected that Charles was too. Regionally, most of the support for the king came from Wales and the west and north of England.

What drew all these people together was that they favoured the status quo or existing situation in both politics and religion and disliked and distrusted change, let alone revolution. They were known as **royalists**, but were later sometimes called **Cavaliers**.

A *cavaliere* is an Italian knightly horseman, and the word was at first used against the royalists in abuse, as it implied that the Cavaliers were both military fanatics and Roman Catholics.

Why would the Cavalier's weapon be of little use to him in battle?

Queen Henrietta Maria was the French-born wife of Charles I.

Who were the Roundheads?

Many people chose to oppose the king. There were political, religious and economic reasons why many supported the opposition to the king. In England, opposition to Charles was led by parliament. Just like it does today, parliament consisted of two houses: an elected House of Commons and a hereditary House of Lords. Many members of parliament disliked the king's efforts to rule the country without them and his failure to call parliament, from 1629 to 1640.

They also opposed his high-handed attempts to raise taxation without their consent. They disliked how he had tried to raise an army in Ireland to fight the Scots in 1640, without consulting them. Parliament wanted to control the army through their ability to raise tax to pay for the soldiers and Charles's actions made parliament fear that one day he would try to raise an army against them. Opposition to Charles was not just restricted to the elected House of Commons. A majority of the hereditary House of Lords also opposed him. The Scottish parliament was against him too.

The main reason other people opposed Charles was because of religion. Scottish Presbyterians, English Puritans and Independents of no particular religious group all opposed Charles's attempts to impose the Church of England and its rules and beliefs on them. Charles's marriage and the belief that he sympathised with Catholics added to the opposition as these groups were also fiercely anti-Roman Catholic. They did not want to reverse the Reformation of the previous century and return to Catholic worship. As most of the religious opposition came from those who favoured a purer form of worship, Charles's opponents were often called Puritans, although they actually held a wide range of beliefs, ideas and views.

DETECTIVE WORK

Find out more about parliament by looking at its official website: http://www.parliament.uk You can visit parliament to listen to debates or watch a committee discuss a new law. Free tours of parliament are also available; check up on these on the website.

The Houses of Parliament in 1647, with the Parliament House where MPs sat, on the left, Westminster Hall in the centre, and Westminster Abbey on the right.

John Pym was a leading parliamentary opponent of Charles I.

'But though it must be confessed, that the public safety and liberty wrought very much with most … who adhered to the Parliament, yet it was principally the differences about religious matters that filled up the Parliament's armies, and put the resolution and valour into their soldiers … And all the sober men that I was acquainted with, who were against the Parliament, were wont to say, "The King has the better cause, but the Parliament has the better men".'

Richard Baxter was a member of the Church of England, but supported a more Puritan form of worship. In his memoirs, published in 1696, he was clear about why people supported parliament and were in opposition to the king.

Charles's opponents drew much of their support from merchants and businessmen who disliked Charles's high taxes. This meant that the opposition had great support in the City of London, where business was based, as well as the seaports and across the south of England. The navy and local **militia** – county defence forces – also supported them.

Just like the royalist Cavaliers, the parliamentarians and Puritans who opposed Charles acquired a nickname. The Cavaliers called them **Roundheads**, as many of them wore their hair short and favoured serious, quiet clothes rather than the more colourful, flamboyant wear of the Cavaliers. The nickname wasn't very accurate as many Roundheads wore their hair fashionably long, and were as fun-loving and colourful as the Cavaliers. However, the name stuck.

The official name of the Houses of Parliament is the Palace of Westminster.

🐾 **Why does parliament sit in a palace?**

What battles were fought in the civil wars?

To him pudel

Bite him peper

Cavalier Dog

Roundhead Curr

O n 22 August 1642, Charles I officially declared war on the English parliament when he raised his standard (banner) at Nottingham. His royalist army consisted of men from Wales and northern England, where his support was strongest, as well as from other groups loyal to the king.

The parliamentary side had no army, but did have control over most of the local militia. The parliamentary leaders quickly raised an army, led by the Earl of Essex, mainly drawn from the south and east of England.

The first major battle was fought on 23 October at Edgehill in Warwickshire, but neither side was able to claim victory. Both sides then tried to capture important towns and their supplies of arms and other materials, with major sieges taking place at Hull, Newark, Reading, York, Chester, Bristol, Gloucester and Plymouth. Charles and the royalists failed to capture London, as a parliamentary army turned back their army at Turnham Green, west of the city, on 13 November 1642. This failure to capture the capital would prove to be important. Further battles also took

This contemporary cartoon shows the two sides throwing insults at each other. The names Cavalier and Roundhead were quickly in use as terms of abuse.

DETECTIVE WORK

Find out if there are any civil war battle sites in your area, or if your town or city was besieged during the war. Your local museum might have an exhibit about the war in your area. You might find this website useful: http://www.british-civil-wars.co.uk/military/index.htm

place across southern and central England in 1642 and 1643, the parliamentary side winning a major victory in Newbury, Berkshire in September 1643, while the royalists won battles in the north and west. Many battles were no more than small-scale skirmishes, and often ended with no result.

Both sides in the war now **conscripted** (forced) men into their armies to increase their numbers. The armies also looked for support in Ireland and Scotland. In September 1643, the various groups of Irish Catholic rebels made peace with the king, allowing his army to return to fight in England. In response, parliament came to an agreement with the Scots. This meant that both sides, the royalists with the Irish Catholics and the parliamentarians with the Scots, had larger armies to fight with. In January 1644, a Scottish army invaded England to fight the king. At first the royalists won the battles, but when the two sides met on 2 July at Marston Moor in Yorkshire, the royalists suffered a heavy defeat. In Scotland, the king had better luck when an Irish army invaded the country and defeated the king's opponents at Tibbermore outside Perth.

The two sides fight at Edgehill in October 1642.

🐾 **What is the name of the flag the soldiers are fighting over in the picture above?**

The Battle of Marston Moor in July 1644, was a major victory for the parliamentary side.

'We lost … two captains and some soldiers, but we took … some colonels and some of their officers, while sundry [several] of their chief officers were killed. We slew more than two thousand of them, took fifteen hundred prisoners, twenty cannon, which was all they had, all their ammunition, all their baggage, ten thousands arms … and many horse cornets.'

Major General James Lumsden, fighting for parliament at Marston Moor, 1644, gave a good account of the barbarity of some of the battles. A 'horse cornet' is a low-ranking **cavalry** officer in the army.

What was the New Model Army?

Both sides suffered from poor leadership and were disunited. Charles was not a strong leader, as he was unable to think quickly or act decisively and did not inspire trust from his men. He did, however, have the support of most of the rich landowners, who raised private armies on his behalf. The commanders of these armies often failed to work together, and Charles could not provide any effective coordination between them. Prince Rupert, his nephew, proved to be the only effective royalist military leader.

Parliament suffered from the same problems, as its military leaders often failed to work well together. Its armies were split into too many military units and there were too many officers, but not enough normal soldiers. Worse still, parliament gave its armies confusing instructions. It was clear that the MPs weren't effective leaders of the army and that they needed to be removed and the army reorganized.

The New Model Army gathers outside royalist-held Oxford.

DETECTIVE WORK

Find out more about the New Model Army, how it formed and how it was run, on http:// www. british-civilwars.co.uk/ glossary/new-model army.htm. This site has lots of information about the military leaders and the civil war in general.

The Battle of Naseby in June 1645 was the first major victory for the New Model Army.

Cromwell's troops line up ready to fight the Battle of Naseby.

The man who managed to achieve this reorganization was Oliver Cromwell, a MP from Huntingdon. In December 1644, he forced parliament to accept the Self-Denying Ordinance, which stated that membership of parliament was incompatible with military command, with the sole exception of himself. In February 1645, parliament then merged all existing armies into a New Model Army, with Sir Thomas Fairfax as leader and Cromwell as his deputy-in-charge of the cavalry (the soldiers fighting on horseback).

Entry into the New Model Army was based on a man's ability as a soldier rather than on his position within society. If he was skilled enough in battle, he could become an officer. One of the leading officers in the New Model Army was a butcher. The removal of any social barriers meant that the New Model Army was open to new ideas and social class meant nothing. Cromwell held strong religious views and he wanted men in the new force who were equally religious. It was not unusual for the men in the New Model Army to sing psalms just before going into battle. Discipline was strict and the training was thorough.

The New Model Army was based on lightly armed cavalry. Soldiers wore thick leather jerkins (close-fitting jackets without sleeves) for protection, as full armour would slow down their horses. These horses were the key to the success of the New Model Army as they allowed the soldiers to attack with speed and surprise, hitting the enemy hard and decisively and then moving on. Prince Rupert nicknamed the soldiers the 'Ironsides' as they cut through the enemy with ease. The first proper use of the New Model Army was in June 1645, at Naseby in Northamptonshire, where the royalist army was severely beaten. Further royalist defeats at Chester and Bristol, and the refusal of the Welsh to supply more troops to the king, meant that the end of the civil war seemed to be in sight.

> 'The Army was New Modelled and a new General was proposed to command it. For which, by the votes of the two Houses of Parliament, myself was nominated though most unfit and so far from desiring it … I was induced to receive the command.'

Sir Thomas Fairfax was the son of a member of the House of Lords but supported parliament against the king. In 1645, he became the commander of the New Model Army.

What were the political and religious debates?

In 1641, parliament abolished the **Court of High Commission**, a church court that Charles had used to suppress opposition to his rule. This court had controlled the press; its abolition meant the end of press censorship. Now anything could be published, even if it was in opposition to the king. The result was that many new newspapers were published, each one arguing its case: parliamentary papers in London and royalist papers in Oxford, where the king's headquarters were. Radical religious and political groups used the new freedom to produce their own pamphlets. As a result, a lively debate sprang up across the country.

John Lilburne was a leading member of the Levellers.

The main debate that overtook the country was about religion and the role of the state-run Church of England. Most people on the parliamentary side wanted to abolish church government by bishops and introduce the Presbyterian system used in Scotland, where members of the church elected their own ministers. Another group known as the Independents wanted to abolish the state church altogether and allow church members to organize themselves as they chose.

🐾 How did the Levellers get their name?

The Putney Debates took place in a church in southwest London. A plaque on the church wall commemorating the event is shown on the opposite page.

The Independents shared many beliefs with the Levellers, a radical political group that grew up in the early 1640s. The Levellers drew their support from working people and from within the ranks of the army.

The main political and religious debates took place inside the New Model Army. The parliament had tried to disband the army in 1647 when fighting had ended and the king had been captured. The soldiers of the New Model Army were outraged at this attempt and the soldiers elected 'agitators' or representatives to make their case, circulate petitions, and campaign for back pay and other rights, such as compensation for army widows. All these debates came to a head in October 1647, when the leaders of the army, the agitators and the Levellers met in St Mary's Church, Putney, west London, to debate the future government and religion of England. The Levellers proposed democratic government, votes for all men (but not women), abolition of the House of Lords, and the establishment of a **republic**. Many other radical proposals were also put forward until the debates ended in November. By then, the political world was in turmoil. Many felt their whole world had been turned upside down.

'For really I think that the poorest he that is in England has a life to live as the greatest he; and therefore truly, sir, I think it clear that every man that is to live under a government ought first by his own consent to put himself under that government; and I do think that the poorest man in England is not at all bound in a strict sense to that government that he has not had a voice to put himself under.'

During the Putney Debates, 29 October 1647, Colonel Rainsborough put forward the case for the Levellers.

In this place
OLIVER CROMWELL
the General Council
of the Army and elected
soldiers of the regiments
held the Putney Debates,
the first recorded
public discussion of
democratic principles.
28 October : 9 November
1647
Presented by the
Cromwell Association
November 1982

DETECTIVE WORK

Find out more about the Putney Debates and their importance in English history on http://www.british-civilwars.co.uk /glossary/putney-debates.htm. Visit St Mary's Church (left) to see where they took place; the church has been much altered since the debates took place but you can still imagine what it was like to have sat in the church and debated the future government of England.

Why did the army leaders seize control?

After the royalist defeat at Naseby in June 1645, the king's position was seriously weakened. Further defeats in both England and Scotland meant that he now controlled only Ireland, parts of Wales and western England. The only way Charles could survive was to attempt to divide his enemies and hope that one of them changed sides to support him.

On 5 May 1646, Charles rode in disguise to the Scottish army camp at Newark in Nottinghamshire and surrendered to the Scots. This attempt to get the Scots to join his forces did not work as the Scots would only negotiate alongside the English parliament, and the king would not agree to do this. The Scots chose to hand the king over to parliament and withdrew from negotiations in January 1647. At this stage, events got very complicated, as all those opposed to the king were divided and were not sure what to do next.

Parliament had tried to disband the New Model Army because the fighting was over and it did not have enough money to pay the troops. Many in the army were outraged at the attempt to disband the troops and responded by seizing the king themselves in June 1647. Led by Oliver Cromwell, the army then tried to negotiate directly with the king. Charles rejected Cromwell's and the army's proposals and was eventually imprisoned at Carisbrooke Castle

'Abundance of the common troopers, and many of the officers, I found to be honest, sober, orthodox men ... But a few proud, self-conceited, hot-headed sectaries had got into the highest places ... and by their very heat and activity bore down on the rest, or carried them along with them ... I perceived that they took the King for a tyrant and an enemy, and really intended absolutely to master him, or to ruin him, and that they thought if they might fight against him they may kill or conquer him.'

Richard Baxter went to visit some friends who had fought for the New Model Army at Naseby and was horrified at what he heard and saw. A sectary is a member of a radical religious sect or political group.

After the Battle of Preston in August 1648, the defeated Scots were pursued from the battlefield by Cromwell's army.

on the Isle of Wight. There he then managed to negotiate an agreement with the Scots. Charles agreed to establish a Presbyterian church in England and the Scots then agreed that they would send an army to support Charles and put him back in power.

The English parliament voted in January 1648 to end all negotiations with the king and once again prepared for war. However, many soldiers disliked Cromwell and the New Model Army's leaders dominating parliament. They also thought that the king's agreement with the Scots was acceptable and that negotiations with him should continue. In February, soldiers in Pembroke Castle in Wales rose in revolt against the army leadership and in support of the king instead. Within a few months, the revolt had spread across South Wales and into England. The army leadership reacted quickly and crushed the English rebels at Maidstone, Kent in June, and at Colchester, Essex in August. Oliver Cromwell and his supporters crushed a rebellion in Wales in July and then defeated the invading Scots, who were supporting the king, at Preston, Lancashire in August.

This second brief civil war was now over with the army and Cromwell in full control and the rebels defeated. The question of what to do with the king was now more urgent than ever.

While imprisoned in Carisbrook Castle by the army, Charles I continued to negotiate with any potential ally he could find.

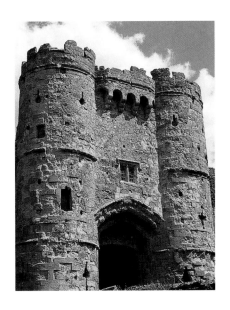

🐾 **Why was Carisbrooke Castle a safe place to keep the king?**

Why was the king executed?

After the second civil war ended in the royalist defeat at Preston in August 1648, a decision had to be made about the king. The army controlled the country and wanted no more negotiations with Charles. Parliament, however, hoped that a defeated Charles would finally come to his senses and negotiate an end to the war. The parliamentarians, therefore, reopened negotiations on the same terms they had offered previously.

The army had had enough of negotiating with the king. On 20 November 1648, they submitted a Remonstrance or ultimatum to parliament, demanding that, 'the capital and grand authors of our troubles, the person of the king ... may be speedily brought to justice for the treason, blood and mischief he is guilty of.' When parliament ignored this demand, the army occupied London and sent Colonel Pride, to evict from parliament those MPs who disagreed with it and wished to continue negotiations with the king.

King Charles walks from St.James's Palace to his place of execution in Whitehall.

'*Truly I deserve [the people's] liberty and freedom as much as anybody: but I must tell you, that their liberty and freedom consists in having government of those laws, by which their life and their goods may be most their own; it is not for having a share in government, that is nothing pertaining to them. A subject and sovereign are clean different things ...*'

Charles delivered a farewell speech on the scaffold just before he died.

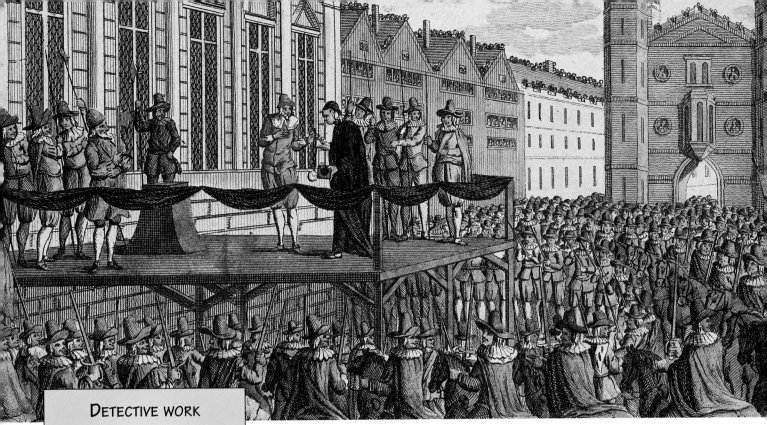

DETECTIVE WORK

Charles I is the only British king to have been put on trial and executed. Find out more about his trial at http://www.british-civilwars.co.uk/glossary/trial-king-charles.htm. You can visit the Banqueting House, which is in Whitehall, just across the road from 10 Downing Street, home of the prime minister.

🐾 How was Charles executed?

Charles was executed on a scaffold (above) outside the Banqueting House in Whitehall (below).

In effect, the army's generals had mounted a military **coup** against the elected parliament by removing all those MPs that disagreed with them and leaving a rump of MPs that agreed with them to run the country. The **Rump Parliament**, as it became known, moved quickly to carry out the army's wishes and try the king. It set up a High Court of Justice and changed the law of high treason to make it an offence to 'levy war against the Parliament and Kingdom of England.' The existing law stated that it was treason to fight against the king, which Charles obviously could not have done!

The trial of Charles I started on 21 January 1649. The formal charge stated that 'Charles Stuart, King of England, you are accused on behalf of the Commons of England of divers high crimes and treasons.' Charles, however, refused to recognise the court at all and argued with his opponents with great skill. He voiced a powerful argument, but in the end, this was a show trial that could only have one result. On 27 January, Charles was found guilty of high treason and sentenced to death, although only 59 of the 135 commissioners or judges who heard his case would sign the death warrant. Three days later, on 30 January, Charles was led to the scaffold erected outside the Banqueting House in Whitehall, and executed.

Who replaced the king?

The execution of Charles solved one immediate problem but it created many other problems. Charles had been king of three kingdoms – England and Wales, Scotland, Ireland – but it was the English parliament that had tried and executed him in the name of the people of England only and not the other kingdoms. Not surprisingly, the Scots and the Irish were outraged, and promptly declared his son, Charles II, as king.

In this contemporary cartoon Oliver Cromwell is cutting down the royal oak of Brittayne (Britain).

The Rump Parliament in London moved quickly to sort out the mess it had created. It abolished the monarchy and it also abolished the hereditary House of Lords. The Rump Parliament set up a Council of State, headed by Oliver Cromwell, to run the country instead. In May 1649, it declared England and Wales a 'Commonwealth and free state', in other words a republic. The new republic had many enemies. An uprising in the army by soldiers in favour of the Levellers, some of whom had been imprisoned for protesting against army rule, was quickly crushed. All remaining royalist opposition was also crushed.

The main military threat came from Ireland, where royalists and Catholics rose in revolt and from where royalist ships were using Irish ports to attack the new English republic's ships. In August 1649, Cromwell landed in Ireland and with great savagery besieged the towns of Drogheda and Wexford before finally defeating the Irish in June 1650. Cromwell then returned to face the Scots. He defeated their army at Dunbar in Lothian in September 1650 and then, when a new Scottish army led by Charles II invaded England, Cromwell defeated them again at Worcester in July 1651.

With the Irish and Scots defeated, the English parliament was now in charge, ruling both Scotland and Ireland. For the first time ever, the British Isles had one government and one parliament, although both were English and run only by Englishmen.

🐾 **Why was Cromwell shown cutting down an oak tree (opposite)?**

The statue of Oliver Cromwell stands outside the Houses of Parliament in London.

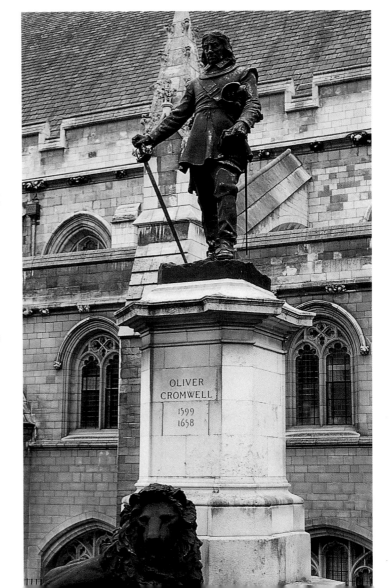

How did Cromwell almost become king?

The parliament that sat after December 1648 was known as the Rump Parliament, because it was the 'rump', what was left over from the original Long Parliament that had sat since 1640. There had been no new elections since 1640, so the Rump's members were not very representative of the country. They had also failed to carry out much-needed reforms, or even raise enough taxation to pay the army's wages.

On 20 April 1653, Oliver Cromwell decided to act. He and a group of soldiers entered the House of Commons and expelled its members. Once again, the army had mounted a coup. The council of leading army officers now nominated a new parliament with members drawn from all four parts of the British Isles, the first time this had ever happened. It was called the 'Barebones' Parliament, after one of its members, Praise-God Barbon or Barebone, but it was no better than its **predecessor** and collapsed at the end of the year.

In its place, Cromwell and his supporters drew up a written **constitution** for the first time in Britain. This constitution was known as the Instrument of Government. It set up the Protectorate uniting the British Isles for the first time under a single government and parliament. Cromwell became Lord Protector, but when the new parliament attacked his role, it was dissolved in 1655. A royalist revolt created further chaos, so in 1655, Cromwell appointed 11 major-generals from the army to run the country. This

In this contemporary woodcut, Oliver Cromwell is shown with other parliamentarians sitting with the devil, as many people thought that Cromwell and his supporters were evil people.

'You have sat here too long for any good you have been doing. Depart, I say, and let us have done with you. In the name of God, go!'

On 20 April 1653, Oliver Cromwell entered the House of Commons and expelled the remaining members of the Rump Parliament.

Oliver Cromwell and a group of soldiers dissolved the **Rump Parliament** in April 1653.

attempt at direct military rule was even more unpopular, and so in 1656, a new parliament was called. It drew up a new constitution, known as the Humble Petition and Advice, that would have made Cromwell king. Cromwell rejected the crown, however, but under this new constitution he was reinstalled as Lord Protector with many of the powers of a monarch.

Even this new system did not work, and so in early 1658, Cromwell dissolved this parliament too. Before he had time to summon a new one, Cromwell died in Whitehall after a brief illness on 3 September 1658. He was only 59, but was worn out by constant criticism: from believers in the republic who thought he had betrayed their ideas and become a monarch, and by royalists who believed he had taken the throne from the rightful king.

🐾 **Who is the man sitting at the back of the Parliament chamber (above)?**

Why was the king restored to the throne?

After Oliver Cromwell's death in 1658, his son Richard took over as Lord Protector. Richard lacked support in the country, and in April 1659, was forced by the army to dismiss parliament when it began to criticise the army's role in government. At this point, Richard resigned, leaving the army in control of the country once again.

'If the general distraction and confusion which is spread over the whole kingdom doth not awaken all men to a desire and longing that those wounds which have so many years been kept bleeding may be bound up, all we can say will be to no purpose.'

On 4 April 1660, Charles II issued the Declaration of Breda.

The army recalled the old Rump Parliament – only 78 of those who were first elected in 1640 were still alive and only 42 actually turned up – but its members too criticized the army. The army then dismissed parliament and set up a Committee of Safety consisting of 23 military men and civilians chosen by them.

At this point, the country erupted in protest, with riots in London and other cities. Merchants and others refused to pay their taxes until parliament was recalled. The army backed down and recalled the Rump Parliament, which received initial support from General Monck, commander of the army in Scotland. But when he saw how little real support it had in the country, he managed in February 1660 to reverse the **purge** of 1648 and bring back those MPs who had been expelled from the **Long Parliament** on the condition they voted to dissolve parliament and hold new elections. This they duly did.

Monck and others now realised that the only way the country could be governed well was to restore the **monarchy**. He therefore opened negotiations with Charles II, who was in exile in Breda in the Netherlands. In April, Charles II issued a declaration promising a general pardon to republicans and limited religious freedom. He also agreed to rely on the advice of parliament.

When the new parliament met, it agreed on 5 May 1660 to restore Charles II to the throne. On 25 May, Charles landed at Dover, reaching London four days later. The king was back, the monarchy now restored and Britain's experiment with a republican government was over.

DETECTIVE WORK

Charles II was a colourful king and was known as the Merry Monarch. Find out more about him and his reign on: http://www.spartacus.schoolnet.co.uk/STUcharles2.htm

In May 1660 Charles II landed at Dover in Kent, the first time he had set foot on English soil for almost nine years.

How did the civil wars change things?

Although Charles II returned to the throne in 1660, debate about the civil wars continued. The wars killed his father and gave Britain its first and only republican government. What really caused the wars and what effect did they have?

The most obvious way to look at the wars is as a clash between a hereditary king and an elected parliament, between a king who believed in his divine right to rule by himself and a parliament that represented the people over whom he ruled. You can also see the wars as a constitutional crisis in, which one king tried to rule three separate kingdoms and impose his views on all three, despite their different laws and religions. This has been a consistent theme in British politics ever since, as relationships between the dominant England and the smaller but independent-minded Scotland and Ireland often cause political and sometimes military conflict right up to the present day.

The civil wars can also be seen as a religious conflict. The king wanted to impose his religious views on the entire nation, while his three kingdoms wanted to worship in their own way. Today, religious views are held less strictly in Britain, but then they dominated everyday life. England and Wales had an **Episcopalian** church, that is a state church governed by bishops, while Scotland was Presbyterian and Ireland largely Roman Catholic. Charles was very religious and believed in the Episcopalian Church of England. The Scots and Irish resented his attempts to remodel their churches in line with his own views. Many Puritans and Independents in England too disliked any form of established church and also fought for their beliefs, which made the situation all the more complex.

Finally, the wars can be seen as a clash between different social classes, between the old landed aristocracy and a new middle class of merchants, gentry and professional men represented in parliament. There were also those groups, such as the Levellers, who demanded a radical restructuring of society.

When Charles returned as king, he reinstated many of the old royal ceremonies, including the laying of hands on those people suffering with scrofula, a type of tuberculosis, as it was believed that the royal touch could cure illness.

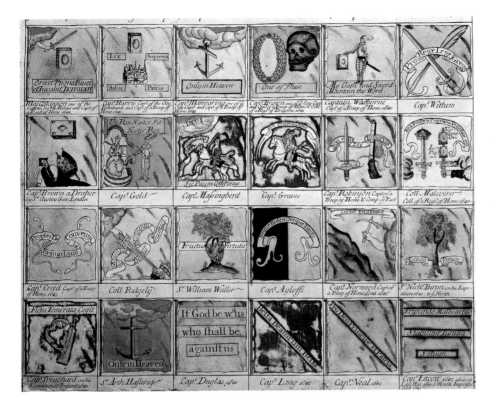

Many of the parliamentarians who fought in the civil wars had their own mottos or sayings that they displayed on their banners.

The effect of the civil wars is still felt today. Britain has remained a monarchy ever since, but its monarchs have always been careful not to upset parliament too much or they could lose their throne, just as James II found out to his cost in 1688, when the throne was taken from him and his daughter, Mary II, replaced him. The army intervened in politics during the civil wars, but it was so disliked that it has never intervened again since. Perhaps the most important effect of the wars has been that Britain has retained its monarch and never had another civil war. And that is an achievement few other European countries can match.

Every year at the state opening of Parliament, Black Rod – a parliamentary official appointed by the monarch – summons the members of the House of Commons to hear the monarch's speech in the House of Lords.

Why are the doors of the House of Commons slammed in Black Rod's face?

Your project

By now you should have collected lots of information about the civil wars. This is the time to think about the sort of project you might like to produce.

You might like to make a profile of one of the two main characters that dominated this period of history, Charles I or Oliver Cromwell. Try writing a short biography or life story of one of them, perhaps setting out events from their point of view and explaining why they acted in the way they did. Or you could write about one of the common soldiers on either the royalist or parliamentary side, showing what it was like to fight a war against your own countrymen. Remember, it is your project, so chose someone who interests you.

Alternatively, you could organize your own trial of Charles I. Set out the charges against the king, and then list the arguments the king could make in his favour against them. You could even appear as a witness for one side! The king is on trial for the most serious crime of high treason: will the evidence presented support the charges against him or are the king's arguments stronger? If the king is found guilty, he will be executed, so the case against him needs to be good.

Charles I delivered a farewell speech on the scaffold before he was executed in London in January 1649.

Project presentation
- Research your project well. Use the Internet and your local library. Is there a nearby society, museum or historical site related to your project? Many of these will also have their own Internet site.
- If you were a time-travelling journalist and could interview your featured person, or appear for the prosecution at the trial, what questions would you ask? Make a list, and then see if you can answer them from your research.
- If you are researching the trial, what questions need to be asked and answered before a verdict can be reached? List them and see if you can answer them all from your research. If the king is found guilty, you could write out the judge's verdict on why he was guilty.
- Collect pictures about your subject and use them to illustrate your biography.

Charles lay down and put his head on a block of wood so that he could be executed.

Glossary

Cavaliers Name given to supporters of Charles I.

cavalry Soldiers who fight on horseback.

conscripted To be enrolled compulsorily or forced to serve in an army.

constitution A written document setting out the principles by which a country is governed and the rights its people enjoy.

coup *Coup d'état*, a sudden violent or illegal seizure of government.

Episcopalian System of church government in which the king appoints bishops, who in turn appoint the ministers.

hereditary Passing down a title, office or land through the generations of a family, usually from father to son.

Independents Those who wanted to abolish the state church and allow local congregations to decide their own form of worship.

Long Parliament The parliament first elected in November 1640 that sat until it was dismissed by Cromwell in April 1653; after it was purged by Colonel Pride in December 1648, it became known as the Rump Parliament. The Rump was recalled in May 1659 and was joined by its surviving expelled members to reform the Long Parliament in February 1660. It finally dissolved itself in March 1660.

militia Groups of part-time soldiers drawn from a town or county who were called up for military service to deal with local emergencies.

monarchy Form of government with a hereditary king or queen as head of state.

MP Member of Parliament.

predecessor Person who holds an office, such as king, before the present occupant.

Presbyterian System of church government in which church members elect presbyters (ministers).

Protestant A person who does not accept the supremacy of the Roman Catholic Church and worships at a Presbyterian or Episcopal church.

purge To rid a parliament or political group of dissident or troublesome people.

Puritan A person who rejects Episcopal government and believes in a purer, simpler form of worship.

republic System of government in which people elect their head of state and government; opposite of monarchy.

Roman Catholic Church Main Christian church in western Europe, led by the Pope in Rome.

Roundhead Name given to Charles I's opponents.

royalist Supporter of the king.

Rump Parliament See Long Parliament.

Answers

Page 4: Whitehall got its name from the light stone used to build York Place (later Whitehall Palace) and other buildings in the area. However, it could also have got its name from the custom of naming any festival hall 'White-Hall'.

Page 7: During the civil wars, most soldiers fought with muskets, a type of gun against which a sword would have been useless.

Page 9: Until 1512, the royal family lived where parliament is now located. A fire forced them to move out, but the building remained a royal palace. That is why its official title is the Palace of Westminster.

Page 11: Each army flies its own special flag known as a standard to tell troops where their commanders are. Capture the enemy's standard and you were close to winning the battle.

Page 14: Opponents nicknamed them the Levellers because they accused the group of wanting to end all class distinctions and make society more level or equal.

Page 17: Carisbrooke Castle is on the Isle of Wight and thus surrounded by sea, making it difficult for a friendly army to come and rescue Charles.

Page 19: Charles was beheaded with an axe.

Page 21: The oak tree is a symbol of authority and stability, as oak trees can live for years.

Page 23: The man sitting at the back of the Parliament chamber is the Speaker of the House of Commons.

Page 27: In 1642, Charles I entered the House of Commons without permission and attempted to arrest five of its members. Black Rod represents the monarch, so in order to symbollize the independence of the House of Commons from the monarch, the doors of the Commons are slammed in his face and he has to knock three times in order to gain entrance.

Further Information

Books to read
Horrible Histories: Slimy Stuarts by Terry Deary (Scholastic, 1996)
What They Don't Tell You About: Charles I and the Civil War by Bob Fowke (Hodder Children's Books, 2001)
Cavaliers and Roundheads by Simon Adams (Franklin Watts, 2002)

Websites
http://www.bbc.co.uk/history/british/civil_war_revolution/
http://www.channel4.com/history/microsites/H/history/war/index.html
http://www.parliament.uk
http://www.cambridgeshire.gov.uk/leisure/museums/cromwell
Note to parents and teachers: Every effort has been made by the publishers to ensure that these websites are suitable for children. However, because of the nature of the Internet, it is impossible to guarantee that the contents of these sites will not be altered. We strongly advise that Internet access is supervised by a responsible adult.

Places to visit
Houses of Parliament, Westminster, London, SW1A 0AA – Cromwell's statue is outside Parliament.
Trafalgar Square, London, WC2N 5DN – Charles I's statue is in the square.
Banqueting House, Whitehall, London, SW1A 2ER – Charles was executed here.
The Cromwell Museum, Shire Hall, Castle Hill, Cambridgeshire, CB3 0AP.

Index

Numbers in **bold** refer to pictures and captions